CHINESE COOKING

JG PRESS

2059
Published in the USA 1995 by JG Press
Distributed by World Publications, Inc
Copyright © 1994 by Colour Library Books Ltd, Godalming, Surrey
All rights reserved
No part of this book may be reproduced or transmitted in any
form or by any means, electronic or mechanical, including
photocopying, recording, or by any information storage and
retrieval system, without permission in writing from the Publisher.
Printed and Bound in Singapore
ISBN 1-57215-013-0

The JG Press imprint is a trademark of JG Press, Inc.
455 Somerset Avenue
North Dighton, MA 02764

INTRODUCTION

To say China is vast seems a gross oversimplification. But it is this vastness that is the key to unlocking the mysteries of the country's cuisine. Because of the great land area, China has a great range of climates which influence the crops that grow and hence the dishes of the regions. It is usual, for culinary purposes, to divide the country into four regions: North or Peking, South or Cantonese, East or Shanghai, West or Szechuan.

In the North, noodles are eaten more often than rice, because that is the wheat growing region. Rich sauces and meat dishes are featured, as are pancakes and dumplings. From this region comes the legendary Peking duck.

In the South, the weather is warmer and the meals lighter. Stir-fried dishes with crisp vegetables are popular. The salty tang of fermented black beans or oyster sauce lends interest to meat and poultry stir-fries. Rice is the staple rather than wheat noodles.

In the East, rice and noodles compete for popularity. Noodles, combined with vegetables, poultry or sea-food, make a favorite snack in tea houses. Fish, both freshwater and saltwater, are plentiful.

In the West, hearty dishes with a fiery taste are a specialty. The Szechuan peppercorn grows here, with a taste very different from the pepper we in the Western world are used to. The edible tree fungus – cloud ear – is a highly-prized ingredient.

Cooking Chinese food takes only minutes for most recipes, but preparation often involves much slicing and chopping, so it is best to have everything ready to go. Ingredients are generally cut to approximately the same size so that they cook in almost the same length of time. To slice meat to the necessary thinness, use it partially frozen.

Stir-frying is probably the most important Chinese cooking method used in this book. This involves cooking over high heat in a small amount of oil. A wok is best for this, but, if necessary, a large heavy-based frying pan can be used. Woks usually sit on a stand which keeps the base slightly elevated to give greater control over cooking.

Chinese food is becoming more and more popular, but some ingredients may still prove mystifying and in need of definition:

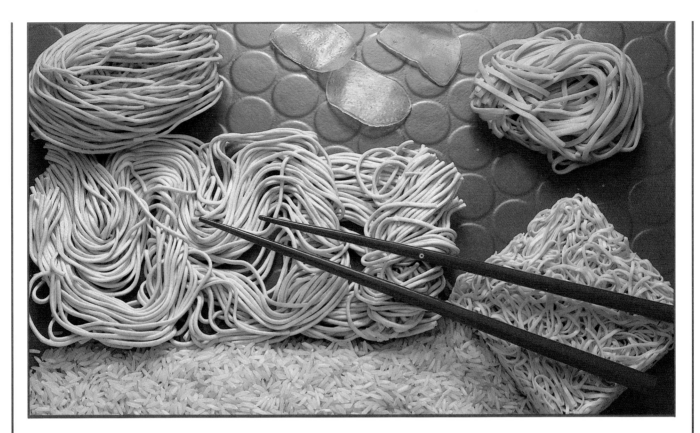

Bamboo shoots – first growth of the bamboo plant, cut just as it emerges from the ground. Crisp, ivory colored and slightly sweet, usually sold canned, sliced or in whole pieces which can be cut to various shapes.

Baby corn – miniature variety of corn. Sold in cans and often available fresh. Needs very brief cooking.

Black beans – used often in Cantonese cooking. Available in pre-prepared sauce or salted to preserve them. Salted beans should be soaked.

Chili peppers – available dried or fresh. Usually red, they are used in Szechuan cooking. Seeds are the hottest part, so remove for less heat.

Chili sauce – available hot or sweet and made from fresh, red chili peppers.

Chinese cabbage – usually refers to Chinese celery cabbage. Some varieties have thicker, whiter spines. Readily available in greengrocers or supermarkets. Smaller, stronger-tasting bok choy is rarely seen outside Chinese markets.

Chinese parsley – also coriander leaves or cilantro. A pungent green herb with a leaf similar to flat parsley.

Five-spice powder – a combination of star anise, anise pepper, fennel, cloves and cinnamon. Use sparingly.

Ginger – knobbly root that must be peeled before use. Use in small amounts, grated or thinly sliced. Also available in powder form or preserved in sugar syrup.

Hoisin sauce – a thick, vegetable-based sauce used often in Chinese barbecue cooking. Useful for stir-fried dishes and as a dipping sauce.

Mushrooms, dried Chinese – brown-black in color, must be soaked for 15-30 minutes before use. Stronger in taste than fresh mushrooms, they also have a chewier texture.

Red bean paste – made from boiled red beans or bean flour mixed with water and flour. Usually sweetened and used in desserts.

Rice wine – available from Chinese groceries, it has a flavor ranging from dry sherry to sweet white wine depending on the variety bought. Substitute either sherry or white wine.

Rice vinegar – made from rice and quite pale in color. Substitute white wine vinegar.

Sesame oil – pressed from sesame seeds it is golden in color with a nutty flavor. Expensive, so use as flavoring at the end of cooking.

Soy sauce – made from fermented soy beans. There are various strength, which will affect the color and flavor of the finished dish.

Star anise – star-shaped seed pod with a liquorice taste. Used in meat, poultry and sweet dishes.

Szechuan peppercorns – also called wild pepper. Not readily available, so substitute black peppercorns.

Water chestnuts – fresh variety is very difficult to obtain. Usually found canned, peeled, sliced or whole. Creamy white in color and crisp in texture.

White radish or mooli – very large, with a delicious, crisp texture and white, translucent appearance. Barely needs cooking.

Wonton skins or wrappers – thin sheets of egg noodle dough in large or small squares. The traditional wrapping for green rolls and dumplings with various stuffings. Can be steamed or cooked in liquid.

Wood or tree ears – grayish-black tree fungus. Sold dried and must be soaked before use.

Yellow beans – whole in brine or in paste or sauce form. Golden brown in color and very salty.

MAKES 12

SPRING ROLLS

One of the most popular Chinese hors
d'oeuvres, these are delicious dipped
in sweet-sour sauce or plum sauce.

Wrappers

1 cup bread flour
1 egg, beaten
Cold water

Filling

8oz pork, trimmed and finely shredded
4oz shrimp, shelled and chopped
4 green onions, finely chopped
2 tsps chopped fresh ginger
4oz Chinese cabbage leaves, shredded
3½oz bean sprouts
1 tbsp light soy sauce
Dash sesame seed oil
1 egg, beaten

1. To prepare the wrappers, sift the flour into a bowl and make a well in the center. Add the beaten egg and about 1 tbsp cold water. Begin beating with a wooden spoon, gradually drawing in the flour from the outside to make a smooth dough. Add more water if necessary.

2. Knead the dough until it is elastic and pliable. Place in a covered bowl and chill for about 4 hours or overnight.

3. When ready to roll out, allow the dough to come back to room temperature. Flour a large work surface well and roll the dough out to about ¼ inch thick.

4. Cut the dough into 12 equal squares and then roll each piece into a larger square about 6x6 inches. The dough should be very thin. Cover while preparing the filling.

5. Cook the pork in a little of the frying oil for about 2-3 minutes. Add the remaining filling ingredients, except the beaten egg, cook for a further 2-3 minutes and allow to cool.

6. Lay out the wrappers on a clean work surface with the point of each wrapper facing you. Brush the edges lightly with the beaten egg.

7. Divide the filling among all 12 wrappers, placing it just above the front point. Fold over the sides like an envelope.

8. Then fold over the point until the filling is completely covered, Roll up as for a jelly roll. Press all the edges to seal well.

9. Heat the oil in a deep fat fryer or in a deep pan to 375°F. Depending upon the size of the fryer, place in 2-4 spring rolls and fry until golden brown on both sides. The rolls will float to the surface when one side has browned and should be turned over. Drain thoroughly on paper towels and serve hot.

Step 7 Fill the dough and fold up sides like an envelope before rolling up.

Cook's Notes

 Time
Preparation takes about 50 minutes for the wrapper dough, the filling and for rolling up. Dough must be allowed to rest for at least 4 hours before use. Cooking takes about 20 minutes.

 Serving Ideas
Serve with a sauce dip. Sweet and sour sauce or hot mustard sauce are available bottled from specialty shops and Chinese supermarkets.

 Freezing
Rolls may be frozen uncooked. Line a baking sheet with plastic wrap, place on the rolls and freeze until nearly solid. Wrap each roll individually, place in a large plastic bag, seal, label and freeze for up to 2 months. Defrost completely before frying.

SERVES 4-6

HOT & SOUR SOUP

A very warming soup, this is a favorite
in winter in Peking. Add chili sauce and
vinegar to suit your taste.

2oz pork
3 dried Chinese mushrooms, soaked in boiling water for
　　5 minutes and chopped
2oz peeled, uncooked shrimp
5 cups chicken stock
1oz bamboo shoots, sliced
3 green onions, shredded
Salt and pepper
1 tbsp sugar
1 tsp dark soy sauce
½ tsp light soy sauce
1-2 tsps chili sauce
1½ tbsps vinegar
Dash sesame seed oil and rice wine or sherry
1 egg, well beaten
2 tbsps water mixed with 1 tbsp cornstarch

1. Trim any fat from the pork and slice it into shreds about
2 inches long and less than ¼ inch thick.

2. Soak the mushrooms in boiling water until softened.
Place the pork in a large pot with the shrimp and stock.
Bring to the boil and then reduce the heat to allow to simmer
gently for 4-5 minutes. Add all the remaining ingredients
except for the egg and cornstarch and water mixture. Cook
a further 1-2 minutes over low heat.

3. Remove the pan from the heat and add the egg
gradually, stirring gently until it forms threads in the soup.

4. Mix a spoonful of the hot soup with the cornstarch and
water mixture and add to the soup, stirring constantly.

5. Bring the soup back to simmering point for 1 minute to
thicken the cornstarch. Serve immediately.

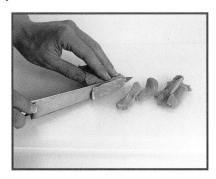

Step 1 Cut the pork into thin shreds, long enough to fit comfortably into a soup spoon.

Step 2 Soak the dry mushrooms in boiling water for 5 minutes until they soften and swell. Remove the stalks before chopping.

Step 3 Pour the egg into the hot soup and stir gently to form threads.

Cook's Notes

Time
Preparation takes about 25 minutes, cooking takes 7-8 minutes.

Preparation
Vary the amount of chili sauce to suit your own taste.

Variation
Hot and Sour Soup is very versatile. Substitute other ingredients such as chicken, crabmeat, bean sprouts, spinach or green cabbage.

Watchpoint
The soup must be hot enough to cook the egg when it is added, but not so hot that the egg sets immediately.

MAKES 12

POT STICKER DUMPLINGS

So called because they are fried in very little
oil, they will stick unless they are brown and
crisp on the bottom before they are steamed.

Dumpling Pastry

1½ cups all-purpose flour
½ tsp salt
3 tbsps oil
Boiling water

Filling

4oz finely ground pork or chicken
4 water chestnuts, finely chopped
3 green onions, finely chopped
½ tsp five spice powder
1 tbsp light soy sauce
1 tsp sugar
1 tsp sesame oil

Step 3 Place a mound of filling on half of each dough circle.

1. Sift the flour and salt into a large bowl and make a well in the center. Pour in the oil and add enough boiling water to make a pliable dough. Add about 4 tbsps water at first and begin stirring with a wooden spoon to gradually incorporate the flour. Add more water as necessary. Knead the dough for about 5 minutes and allow to rest for 30 minutes.

2. Divide the dough into 12 pieces and roll each piece out to a circle about 6 inches in diameter.

3. Mix all the filling ingredients together and place a mound of filling on half of each circle. Fold over the top and press the edges together firmly. Roll over the joined edges using a twisting motion and press down to seal.

4. Pour about ⅛ inch of oil in a large frying pan, preferably cast iron. When the oil is hot, add the dumplings flat side down and cook until nicely browned.

5. When the underside is brown, add about ⅓ cup water to the pan and cover it tightly. Continue cooking gently for about 5 minutes, or until the top surface of dumplings is steamed and appears cooked. Serve immediately.

Step 3 Fold over the dough and press edges to seal in filling.

Step 3 Twist the edges together to seal firmly.

Cook's Notes

Time
Preparation takes about 50 minutes including the standing time for the dough. Cooking takes about 10-20 minutes.

Preparation
The pan used for cooking must have a flat base. Do not use a wok.

Watchpoint
Make sure the dumplings are brown and crisp on the bottom before adding the water otherwise they really will be pot stickers!

SERVES 4-6

CRAB & SWEETCORN SOUP

Creamy sweetcorn and succulent crabmeat
combine to make a velvety rich soup. Whisked
egg whites add an interesting texture.

3½ cups chicken or fish stock
12oz cream style corn
4oz crabmeat
Salt and pepper
1 tsp light soy sauce
2 tbsps cornstarch
3 tbsps water or stock
4 green onions for garnish
2 egg whites, whisked
4 green onions for garnish

Step 3 Whisk the egg whites until soft peaks form and stir into the hot soup.

Step 2 Mix the cornstarch and water together with some of the hot soup and return the mixture to the pan.

1. Bring the stock to the boil in a large pan. Add the corn, crabmeat, seasoning and soy sauce. Allow to simmer for 4-5 minutes.

2. Mix the cornstarch and water or stock and add a spoonful of the hot soup. Return the mixture to the soup and bring back to the boil. Cook until the soup thickens.

3. Whisk the egg whites until soft peaks form. Stir into the hot soup just before serving.

4. Slice the onions thinly on the diagonal and scatter over the top to serve.

Cook's Notes

 Time
Preparation takes about 10 minutes, cooking takes about 8-10 minutes.

 Preparation
Adding the egg whites is optional.

 Watchpoint
Do not allow the corn and the crab to boil rapidly; they will both toughen.

 Economy
Use crab sticks instead of crabmeat.

 Variation
Chicken may be used instead of the crabmeat and the cooking time increased to 10-12 minutes.

SERVES 6-8

WONTON SOUP

Probably the best-known Chinese soup,
this recipe uses pre-made wonton
wrappers for ease of preparation.

20-24 wonton wrappers
2 tbsps chopped Chinese parsley
3oz finely ground chicken or pork
3 green onions, finely chopped
1 inch piece fresh ginger, peeled and grated
1 egg, lightly beaten
5 cups chicken stock
1 tbsps dark soy sauce
Dash sesame oil
Salt and pepper
Chinese parsley or watercress for garnish

Step 2 Place a spoonful of filling on half of each wrapper

Step 3 Fold over the tops and press firmly with the fingers to seal.

Step 1 Place the wonton wrappers out on a clean surface. Brush edges with beaten egg.

1. Place all the wonton wrappers on a large, flat surface. Mix together the chicken or pork, chopped parsley, green onions and ginger. Brush the edges of the wrappers lightly with beaten egg.

2. Place a small mound of mixture on one half of the wrappers and fold the other half over the top to form a

triangle.

3. Press with the fingers to seal the edges well.

4. Bring the stock to the boil in a large saucepan. Add the filled wontons and simmer 5-10 minutes or until they float to the surface. Add remaining ingredients to the soup, using only the leaves of the parsley or watercress for garnish.

Cook's Notes

 Time
Preparation takes 25-30 minutes and cooking takes about 5-10 minutes.

 Variation
Use equal quantities of crabmeat or shrimp to fill the wontons instead of chicken or pork.

 Buying Guide
Wonton wrappers are sometimes called wonton skins. They are available in speciality shops, delicatessens and Chinese supermarkets. Chinese parsley is also known as coriander or cilantro and is available from greengrocers and supermarkets.

SERVES 4-6

BARBECUED SPARE RIBS

Although Chinese barbecue sauce is nothing like
the tomato-based American-style sauce, these
ribs are still tasty cooked on an outdoor grill.

4lbs fresh spare-ribs
3 tbsps dark soy sauce
6 tbsps hoisin sauce (Chinese barbecue sauce)
2 tbsps dry sherry
¼ tsp five spice powder
1 tbsp brown sugar
4-6 green onions for garnish

Step 2 Cut both ends of the onions into thin strips, leaving the middle whole.

Step 1 Trim the root ends and the green tops from the onions.

Step 3 Place in ice water and leave to stand 4 hour or overnight until the ends curl.

1. First prepare the garnish. Trim the root ends and the dark green tops from the onions.

2. Cut both ends into thin strips, leaving about ½ inch in the middle uncut.

3. Place the onions in ice water for several hours or overnight for the ends to curl up.

4. Cut the spare-ribs into one-rib pieces. Mix all the remaining ingredients together, pour over the ribs and stir to coat evenly. Allow to stand for 1 hour.

5. Put the spare-rib pieces on a rack in a roasting pan containing 2 cups water and cook in a preheated 350°F oven for 30 minutes. Add more hot water to the pan while cooking, if necessary.

6. Turn the ribs over and brush with the remaining sauce. Cook 30 minutes longer, or until tender. Serve garnished with the onion brushes.

Cook's Notes

Time
Preparation takes about 45 minutes. The onion brushes must soak for at least 4 hours and the ribs must marinate for 1 hour. Cooking takes about 1 hour.

Preparation
If the ribs are small and not very meaty, cut into two-rib pieces before cooking, then into one-rib pieces just before serving.

Cook's Tip
The ribs may be prepared in advance and reheated at the same temperature for about 10 minutes.

SERVES 8

SESAME CHICKEN WINGS

This is an economical appetizer that is
also good as a cocktail snack or as a
light meal with stir-fried vegetables.

12 chicken wings
1 tbsp salted black beans
1 tbsp water
1 tbsp oil
2 cloves garlic, crushed
2 slices fresh ginger, cut into fine shreds
3 tbsps soy sauce
1½ tbsps dry sherry or rice wine
Large pinch black pepper
1 tbsp sesame seeds

1. Cut off and discard the wing tips. Cut between the joint
to separate into two pieces.

2. Crush the beans and add the water. Leave to stand.

3. Heat the oil in a wok and add the garlic and ginger. Stir
briefly and add the chicken wings. Cook, stirring, until
lightly browned, about 3 minutes. Add the soy sauce and
wine and cook, stirring, about 30 seconds longer. Add the
soaked black beans and pepper.

4. Cover the wok tightly and allow to simmer for about 8-10
minutes. Uncover and turn the heat to high. Continue
cooking, stirring until the liquid is almost evaporated and
the chicken wings are glazed with sauce. Remove from the

Step 1 Use a
knife or scissors
to cut through
thick joint and
separate the wing
into two pieces.

Step 3 Fry garlic
and ginger briefly,
add the chicken
wings and cook,
stirring, until
lightly browned.

heat and sprinkle on sesame seeds. Stir to coat completely
and serve. Garnish with green onions or Chinese parsley, if
desired.

Cook's Notes

Time
Preparation takes about 25
minutes, cooking takes about
13-14 minutes.

Watchpoint
Sesame seeds pop slightly as
they cook.

Cook's Tip
You can prepare the chicken
wings ahead of time and
reheat them. They are best reheated in
the oven for about 5 minutes at 350°F.

Serving Ideas
To garnish with scallion
brushes, trim the roots and
green tops of green onions and cut
both ends into thin strips, leaving the
middle intact. Place in ice water for
several hours or overnight for the cut
ends to curl up. Drain and use to
garnish.

SERVES 4-6

QUICK FRIED SHRIMP

Prepared with either raw or cooked
shrimp, this is an incredibly delicious
appetizer that is extremely easy to cook.

2lbs cooked shrimp in their shells
2 cloves garlic, crushed
1 inch piece fresh ginger, finely chopped
1 tbsp chopped fresh Chinese parsley (coriander)
3 tbsps oil
1 tbsp rice wine or dry sherry
1½ tbsps light soy sauce
Chopped green onions to garnish

Step 2 Peel the shells from the shrimp, leaving only the tail ends on.

Step 1 Carefully pull the head of the shrimp away from the body.

1. Shell the shrimp except for the very tail ends. Place the shrimp in a bowl with the remaining ingredients, except for the garnish, and leave to marinate for 30 minutes.

2. Heat the wok and add the shrimp and their marinade. Stir-fry briefly to heat the shrimp.

3. Chop the onions roughly or cut into neat rounds. Sprinkle over the shrimp to serve.

Cook's Notes

Time
Preparation takes about 30 minutes for the shrimp to marinate. Cooking takes about 2 minutes.

Watchpoint
Do not overcook the shrimp as they will toughen.

Variation
If uncooked shrimp are available, stir-fry with their marinade until they turn pink.

SERVES 4

EGGPLANT & PEPPER SZECHUAN STYLE

Authentic Szechuan food is fiery hot.
Outside China, restaurants often tone down the taste for Western palates.

1 large eggplant
2 cloves garlic, crushed
1 inch piece fresh ginger, shredded
1 onion, cut into 1 inch pieces
1 small green pepper, seeded, cored and cut into 1 inch pieces
1 small red pepper, seeded, cored and cut into 1 inch pieces
1 red or green chili, seeded, cored and cut into thin strips
½ cup chicken or vegetable stock
1 tsp sugar
1 tsp vinegar
Pinch salt and pepper
1 tsp cornstarch
1 tbsp soy sauce
Dash sesame oil
Oil for cooking

Step 2 Sprinkle lightly with salt and leave on paper towels or in a colander to drain.

Step 1 Cut eggplant in half and lightly score the surface.

1. Cut the eggplants in half and score the surface.

2. Sprinkle lightly with salt and leave to drain in a colander or on paper towels for 30 minutes.

3. After 30 minutes, squeeze the eggplant gently to extract any bitter juices and rinse thoroughly under cold water. Pat dry and cut the eggplant into 1 inch cubes.

4. Heat about 3 tbsps oil in a wok. Add the eggplant and stir-fry for about 4-5 minutes. It may be necessary to add more oil as the eggplant cooks. Remove from the wok and set aside.

5. Reheat the wok and add 2 tbsps oil. Add the garlic and ginger and stir-fry for 1 minute. Add the onions and stir-fry for 2 minutes. Add the green pepper, red pepper and chili pepper and stir-fry for 1 minute. Return the eggplant to the wok along with the remaining ingredients.

6. Bring to the boil, stirring constantly, and cook until the sauce thickens and clears. Serve immediately.

Cook's Notes

Time
Preparation takes about 30 minutes, cooking takes about 7-8 minutes.

Cook's Tip
Lightly salting the aubergine will help draw out any bitterness.

Serving Suggestions
Serve as a vegetarian stir-fry dish with plain or fried rice, or serve as a side dish.

SERVES 4

SPECIAL MIXED VEGETABLES

This dish illustrates the basic stir-frying
technique for vegetables. Use other varieties
for an equally colorful side dish.

1 tbsp oil
1 clove garlic, crushed
1 inch piece fresh ginger, sliced
4 Chinese cabbage leaves, shredded
2oz flat mushrooms, thinly sliced
2oz bamboo shoots, sliced
3 sticks celery, diagonally sliced
2oz baby corn, cut in half if large
1 small red pepper, cored, seeded and thinly sliced
2oz bean sprouts
2 tbsps light soy sauce
Dash sesame oil
Salt and pepper
3 tomatoes, peeled, seeded and quartered

1. Heat the oil in a wok and add the ingredients in the order given, reserving the tomatoes until last.

2. To make it easier to peel the tomatoes, remove the stems and place in boiling water for 5 seconds.

3. Remove from the boiling water with a draining spoon and place in a bowl of cold water. This will make the peels easier to remove. Cut out the core end using a small sharp knife.

4. Cut the tomatoes in half and then in quarters. Use a teaspoon or a serrated edged knife to remove the seeds and the cores.

5. Cook the vegetables for about 2 minutes. Stir in the soy sauce and sesame oil and add the tomatoes. Heat through for 30 seconds and serve immediately.

Step 2 To peel the tomatoes, place them first in a pan of boiling water for 5 seconds. Tomatoes that are very ripe need less time.

Step 3 Place in cold water to stop the cooking. The skin will then peel away easily.

Step 4 Cut into quarters and remove the seeds core and juice with a teaspoon. or use a serrated edged knife.

Cook's Notes

Time
Preparation takes about 25 minutes, cooking takes about 2½-3 minutes.

Variation
Other vegetables such as broccoli flowerets, cauliflower flowerets, pea pods, zucchini or green beans may be used.

Serving Ideas
Serve as a side dish or as a vegetarian main dish with plain or fried rice.

SERVES 4-6

PORK & SHRIMP CHOW MEIN

Chinese chow mein dishes are usually based on noodles, using more expensive ingredients in small amounts. This makes economical everyday fare.

8oz medium dried Chinese noodles
8oz pork fillet, thinly sliced
1 carrot, peeled and shredded
1 small red pepper, cored, seeded and thinly sliced
3oz bean sprouts
2oz pea pods
1 tbsp rice wine or dry sherry
2 tbsps soy sauce
4oz peeled, cooked shrimp

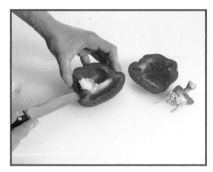

Step 3 Cut peppers in half and remove the cores and seeds. Make sure all the white pith is also removed before slicing thinly.

Step 1 Place whole sheets of noodles into rapidly boiling salted water. Stir as the noodles start to soften.

Step 4 Add the cooked noodles to the other ingredients in the wok and use chopsticks or a spatula to toss over high heat.

1. Cook the noodles in plenty of boiling salted water for about 4-5 minutes. Rinse under hot water and drain thoroughly.

2. Heat the wok and add oil. Stir-fry the pork 4-5 minutes or until almost cooked. Add the carrots to the wok and cook for 1-2 minutes.

3. Core, seed and slice the red pepper and add the remaining vegetables, wine and soy sauce. Cook for about 2 minutes.

4. Add the cooked, drained noodles and shrimp and toss over heat for 1-2 minutes. Serve immediately.

Cook's Notes

Time
Preparation takes about 20 minutes. The noodles take 4-5 minutes to cook and the stir-fried ingredients need to cook for about 5-6 minutes for the pork and about 3 minutes for the vegetables.

Variation
Use green pepper instead of red, or add other vegetables such as baby corn ears, mushrooms or peas.

Buying Guide
Dried Chinese noodles are available in three thicknesses. Thin noodles are usually reserved for soup, while medium and thick noodles are used for fried dishes.

SERVES 2-3

CANTONESE EGG FU YUNG

As the name suggests, this dish is from
Canton. However, fu yung dishes are popular
in many other regions of China, too.

5 eggs
2oz shredded cooked meat, poultry or fish
1 stick celery, finely shredded
4 Chinese dried mushrooms, soaked in boiling water for
　　5 minutes
2oz bean sprouts
1 small onion, thinly sliced
Pinch salt and pepper
1 tsp dry sherry
Oil for frying

Sauce

1 tbsp cornstarch dissolved in 3 tbsps cold water
1 cup chicken stock
1 tsp tomato ketchup
1 tbsp soy sauce
Pinch salt and pepper
Dash sesame oil

1. Beat the eggs lightly and add the shredded meat and celery.

2. Squeeze all the liquid from the dried mushrooms. Remove the stems and cut the caps into thin slices. Add to the egg mixture along with the bean sprouts and onion. Add a pinch of salt and pepper and the sherry and stir well.

3. Heat a wok or frying pan and pour in about 4 tbsps oil. When hot, carefully spoon in about ⅓ cup of the egg mixture.

4. Brown on one side, turn gently over and brown the other side. Remove the cooked patties to a plate and continue until all the mixture is cooked.

5. Combine all the sauce ingredients in a small, heavy-based pan and bring slowly to the boil, stirring continuously until thickened and cleared. Pour the sauce over the Egg Fu Yung to serve.

Step 3 Heat the oil in a wok and spoon in the egg mixture to form patties.

Step 5 Bring sauce ingredients to the boil and cook until thick and clear.

Cook's Notes

Time
Preparation takes 25 minutes, cooking takes about 5 minutes for the patties and 8 minutes for the sauce.

Variation
Use cooked shellfish such as crab, shrimp or lobster, if desired. Fresh mushrooms may be used instead of the dried ones. Divide mixture in half or in thirds and cook one large patty per person.

Economy
Left-over cooked meat such as beef, pork or chicken can be used as an ingredient.

SERVES 6-8

FRIED RICE

A basic recipe for a traditional Chinese accompaniment
to stir-fried dishes, this can be more substantial
with the addition of meat, poultry or seafood.

1lb cooked rice, well drained and dried
3 tbsps oil
1 egg, beaten
1 tbsp soy sauce
2oz cooked peas
2 green onions, thinly sliced
Dash sesame oil
Salt and pepper

Step 2 Add rice and peas on top of egg mixture.

1. Heat a wok and add the oil. Pour in the egg and soy sauce and cook until just beginning to set.

2. Add the rice and peas and stir to coat with the egg mixture. Allow to cook for about 3 minutes, stirring continuously. Add seasoning and sesame oil.

3. Spoon into a serving dish and sprinkle over the green onions.

Step 2 Stir to coat the rice with egg, and toss mixture over heat to separate grains of rice.

Cook's Notes

Time
The rice will take about 10 minutes to cook. Allow at least 20 minutes for it to drain as dry as possible. The fried rice dish will take about 4 minutes to cook.

Variation
Cooked meat, poultry or seafood may be added to the rice along with the peas.

Cook's Tip
The 1lb rice measurement is the cooked weight.

SERVES 4

SHANGHAI NOODLES

In general, noodles are more popular in northern and eastern China, where wheat is grown, than in other parts of the country. Noodles make a popular snack in Chinese tea houses.

3 tbsps oil
4oz chicken breasts
4oz Chinese cabbage
4 green onions, thinly sliced
2 tbsps soy sauce
Freshly ground black pepper
Dash sesame oil
1lb thick Shanghai noodles, cooked

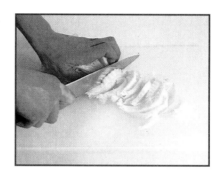

Step 3 Stack up the Chinese leaves and, using a large, sharp knife, cut across into thin strips.

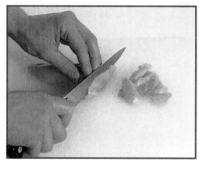

Step 1 Cut the chicken into thin strips across the grain.

Step 3 Toss in the cooked noodles, stir well and heat through.

1. Heat the oil in the wok and add the chicken cut into thin shreds. Stir-fry for 2-3 minutes.

2. Meanwhile, cook the noodles in boiling salted water until just tender, about 6-8 minutes. Drain in a colander and rinse under hot water. Toss in the colander to drain and leave to dry.

3. Add the shredded Chinese cabbage and green onions to the chicken in the wok along with the soy sauce, pepper and sesame oil. Cook about 1 minute and toss in the cooked noodles. Stir well and heat through. Serve immediately.

Cook's Notes

 Time
Preparation takes about 10 minutes, cooking takes 6-8 minutes.

 **Variation**
Pork may be used instead of the chicken. Add fresh spinach, shredded, if desired and cook with the Chinese cabbage.

 Buying Guide
Shanghai noodles are available in Chinese supermarkets and also some delicatessens. If unavailable, substitute tagliatelle or dried Chinese noodles.

SERVES 2

SWEET-SOUR FISH

In China this dish is almost always
prepared with freshwater fish, but
sea bass is also an excellent choice.

1 sea bass, gray mullet or carp, weighing about 2lbs,
  cleaned
1 tbsp dry sherry
Few slices fresh ginger
½ cup sugar
6 tbsps cider vinegar
1 tbsp soy sauce
2 tbsps cornstarch
1 clove garlic, crushed
2 green onions, shredded
1 small carrot, peeled and finely shredded
1oz bamboo shoots, shredded

1. Rinse the fish well inside and out. Make three diagonal
cuts on each side of the fish with a sharp knife.

2. Trim off the fins, leaving the dorsal fin on top.

3. Trim the tail to two neat points.

4. Bring enough water to cover the fish to the boil in a wok.
Gently lower the fish into the boiling water and add the
sherry and ginger. Cover the wok tightly and remove at
once from the heat. Allow to stand 15-20 minutes to let the
fish cook in the residual heat.

5. To test if the fish is cooked, pull the dorsal fin – if it comes
off easily the fish is done. If not, return the wok to the heat
and bring to the boil. Remove from the heat and leave the
fish to stand a further 5 minutes. Transfer the fish to a heated
serving dish and keep it warm. Take all but 4 tbsps of the fish
cooking liquid from the wok. Add the remaining ingredients
including the vegetables and cook, stirring constantly, until
the sauce thickens. Spoon some of the sauce over the fish
to serve and serve the rest separately.

Step 1 Rinse the
fish well and
make three
diagonal cuts on
each side.

Step 2 Using
kitchen scissors,
trim all of the fins
except the dorsal
fin at the top.

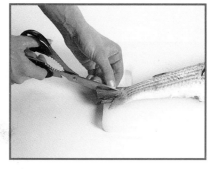

Step 3 Using
kitchen scissors
again, trim the
ends of the tail to
two sharp points.

Cook's Notes

Time
Preparation takes about 25
minutes, cooking takes about
15-25 minutes.

Cook's Tip
The diagonal cuts in the side
of the fish ensure even
cooking.

Variation
If desired, use smaller fish
such as trout or red mullet and
shorten the cooking time to 10-15
minutes.

Preparation
The fish may also be cooked
in the oven in a large roasting
pan or in greased foil sprinkled with
sherry. Cook at 375°F for 10 minutes
per ½ inch thickness, measured
around the middle of the fish.

SERVES 6

SINGAPORE FISH

The cuisine of Singapore was much influenced by
that of China. In turn, the Chinese brought
ingredients like curry powder into their own cuisine.

1lb whitefish fillets
1 egg white
1 tbsp cornstarch
2 tsps white wine
Salt and pepper
Oil for frying
1 large onion, cut into ½ inch-thick wedges
1 tbsp mild curry powder
1 small can pineapple pieces, drained and juice
    reserved, or ½ fresh pineapple, peeled and cubed
1 small can mandarin orange segments, drained and
    juice reserved
1 small can sliced water chestnuts, drained
1 tbsp cornstarch mixed with juice of 1 lime
2 tsps sugar (optional)
Pinch salt and pepper

1. Starting at the tail end of the fillets, skin them using a sharp knife.

2. Slide the knife back and forth along the length of each fillet, pushing the fish flesh along as you go.

3. Cut the fish into even-sized pieces, about 2 inches.

4. Mix together the egg white, cornstarch, wine, salt and pepper. Place the fish in the mixture and leave to stand while heating the oil.

5. When the oil is hot, fry a few pieces of fish at a time until light golden brown and crisp. Remove the fish to paper towels to drain, and continue until all the fish is cooked.

6. Remove all but 1 tbsp of the oil from the wok and add the onion. Stir-fry the onion for 1-2 minutes and add the curry

powder. Cook the onion and curry powder for a further 1-2 minutes. Add the juice from the pineapple and mandarin oranges and bring to the boil.

7. Combine the cornstarch and lime juice and add a spoonful of the boiling fruit juice. Return the mixture to the wok and cook until thickened, about 2 minutes. Taste and add sugar if desired. Add the fruit, water chestnuts and fried fish to the wok and stir to coat. Heat through 1 minute and serve immediately.

Step 2 Hold filleting knife at a slight angle and slide knife along length of fillet in a sawing motion.

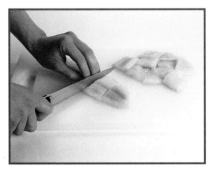

Step 3 Cut fish into even-sized pieces, about 2 inches.

Cook's Notes

 Time
Preparation takes about 25 minutes, cooking takes about 10 minutes.

Variation
Chicken may be used in place of the fish and cooked in the same way. Garnish with Chinese parsley leaves if desired.

 Serving Ideas
Serve with plain rice, fried rice or cooked Chinese noodles.

SERVES 2-4

SNOW PEAS WITH SHRIMP

Snow peas, pea pods and mangetout are
all names for the same vegetable – bright
green, crisp and edible, pods and all.

3 tbsps oil
½ cup split blanched almonds, halved
4oz pea pods
2oz bamboo shoots, sliced
2 tsps cornstarch
2 tsps light soy sauce
¾ cup chicken stock
2 tbsps dry sherry
Salt and pepper
1lb cooked, peeled shrimp

Step 2 Tear stems
downward to
remove strings
from pea pods.

1. Heat the oil in a wok. Add the almonds and cook over moderate heat until golden brown. Remove from the oil and drain on paper towels.

2. To prepare the pea pods, tear off the stems and pull them downwards to remove any strings. If the pea pods are small, just remove the stalks. Add the pea pods to the hot oil and cook for about 1 minute. Remove and set aside with the almonds.

3. Drain all the oil from the wok and mix together the cornstarch and the remaining ingredients, except the shrimp and bamboo shoots. Pour the mixture into the wok and stir constantly while bringing to the boil. Allow to simmer for 1-2 minutes until thickened and cleared. Stir in the shrimp and all the other ingredients and heat through for about 1 minute. Serve immediately.

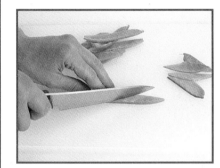

Step 2 If pea
pods are very
large, cut in half
on the diagonal.

Step 3 Add all
the ingredients to
the wok and stir-
fry, tossing with
chopsticks or a
spatula.

Cook's Notes

Time
Preparation takes about 10
minutes, cooking takes
6-8 minutes.

Variation
If using green onions, celery
or water chestnuts, cook with
the pea pods.

Watchpoint
Do not cook the shrimp too
long or on heat that is too high
– they toughen quite easily.

SERVES 6

SZECHUAN FISH

The piquant spiciness of Szechuan pepper is quite different from that of black or white pepper. Beware, though, too much can numb the mouth temporarily!

1lb whitefish fillets
Pinch salt and pepper
1 egg
5 tbsps flour
6 tbsps white wine
Oil for frying
2oz cooked ham, cut in small dice
1 inch piece fresh ginger, finely diced
½-1 red or green chili pepper, cored, seeded and finely diced
6 water chestnuts, finely diced
4 green onions, finely chopped
3 tbsps light soy sauce
1 tsp cider vinegar or rice wine vinegar
½ tsp ground Szechuan pepper (optional)
1 cup light stock
1 tbsp cornstarch dissolved with 2 tbsps water
2 tsps sugar

1. To prepare the garnish, choose unblemished chili peppers with the stems on. Using a small, sharp knife, cut the peppers in strips, starting from the pointed end.

2. Cut down to within ½ inch of the stem end. Rinse out the seeds under cold running water and place the peppers in iced water.

3. Leave the peppers to soak for at least 4 hours or overnight until they open up like flowers.

4. Cut the fish fillets into 2 inch pieces and season with salt and pepper. Beat the egg well and add flour and wine to make a batter. Dredge the fish lightly with flour and then dip into the batter. Mix the fish well.

5. Heat a wok and when hot, add enough oil to deep-fry the fish. When the oil is hot, fry a few pieces of fish at a time, until golden brown. Drain and proceed until all the fish is cooked.

6. Remove all but 1 tbsp of oil from the wok and add the ham, ginger, diced chili pepper, water chestnuts and green onions. Cook for about 1 minute and add the soy sauce and vinegar. If using Szechuan pepper, add at this point. Stir well and cook for a further 1 minute. Remove the vegetables from the pan and set them aside.

7. Add the stock to the wok and bring to the boil. When boiling, add 1 spoonful of the hot stock to the cornstarch mixture. Add the mixture back to the stock and reboil, stirring constantly until thickened.

8. Stir in the sugar and return the fish and vegetables to the sauce. Heat through for 30 seconds and serve at once.

Step 1 Cut the tip of each chili pepper into strips.

Step 3 Allow to soak 4 hours or overnight to open up.

Cook's Notes

Time
Preparation takes about 30 minutes. Chili pepper garnish takes at least 4 hours to soak. Cooking takes about 10 minutes.

Serving Ideas
Serve with plain or fried rice. Do not eat the chili pepper garnish.

$

Buying Guide
Szechuan peppercorns are available in Chinese supermarkets or delicatessens. If not available, substitute extra chili pepper.

KUNG PAO SHRIMP WITH CASHEW NUTS

It is said that Kung Pao invented this dish,
but to this day no one knows who he was!

½ tsp chopped fresh ginger
1 tsp chopped garlic
1½ tbsps cornstarch
¼ tsp bicarbonate of soda
Salt and pepper
¼ tsp sugar
1lb uncooked shrimp
4 tbsps oil
1 small onion, cut into dice
1 large or 2 small zucchini, cut into ½ inch cubes
1 small red pepper, cut into ½ inch cubes
½ cup cashew nuts

Sauce

¾ cup chicken stock
1 tbsp cornstarch
2 tsps chili sauce
2 tsps bean paste (optional)
2 tsps sesame oil
1 tbsp dry sherry or rice wine

1. Mix together the ginger, garlic, 1½ tbsps cornstarch, bicarbonate of soda, salt, pepper and sugar.

2. If the shrimp are unpeeled, remove the peels and the dark vein running along the rounded side. If large, cut in half, Place in the dry ingredients and leave to stand for 20 minutes.

3. Heat the oil in a wok and when hot add the shrimp. Cook, stirring over high heat for about 20 seconds, or just until the shrimp change color. Transfer to a plate.

4. Add the onion to the same oil in the wok and cook for about 1 minute. Add the zucchini and red pepper and cook about 30 seconds.

5. Mix the sauce ingredients together and add to the wok. Cook, stirring constantly, until the sauce is slightly thickened. Add the shrimp and the cashew nuts and heat through completely.

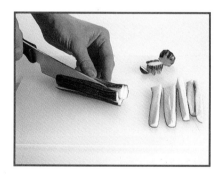

Step 4 To dice the zucchini quickly, top and tail and cut into ½ inch strips.

Step 4 Cut the strips across with a large sharp knife into ½ inch pieces.

Cook's Notes

 Time
Preparation takes about 20 minutes, cooking takes about 3 minutes.

 Variation
If using cooked shrimp, add with the vegetables. Vary amount of chili sauce to suit your taste.

 Serving Ideas
Serve with plain or fried rice.

SERVES 8

PEKING BEEF

In China, meat is often simmered in large earthenware casseroles placed on asbestos mats. A wok is a convenient substitute and the stand does the work of the traditional mat.

2lb sirloin tip or rump roast
1½ cups white wine
2 cups water
2 whole green onions, roots trimmed
1 inch piece fresh ginger
3 star anise
2 tsps sugar
½ cup soy sauce
1 carrot, peeled
2 sticks celery
½ mooli (daikon) radish, peeled

Step 3 Cut the celery into three strips and then into thin strips.

Step 3 Cut the vegetables into 3 inch lengths. To shred carrots, cut each length into thin slices, stack the slices 3-4 at a time and cut through into thin strips with a sharp knife.

1. Place the beef in a wok and add the white wine, water, green onions, ginger and anise. Cover and simmer for about 1 hour.

2. Add the soy sauce and sugar, stir and simmer for 30 minutes longer, or until the beef is tender. Allow to cool in the liquid.

3. Shred all the vegetables finely. Blanch them all, except the green onion, in boiling water for about 1 minute. Rinse under cold water, drain and leave to dry.

4. When the meat is cold, remove it from the liquid and cut into thin slices. Arrange on a serving plate and strain the liquid over it. Scatter over the shredded vegetables and serve cold.

Cook's Notes

Time
Preparation takes about 25 minutes if shredding the vegetables by hand. This can also be done with the fine shredding blade of a food processor. Cooking takes about 1½ hours.

Economy
Because of the long cooking time, less expensive cuts of meat may be used for this dish.

Cook's Tip
If using a rolled roast, remove as much of the fat from the outside as possible. Skim off any fat that rises to the surface of the liquid as it cools, before pouring over the meat to serve.

SERVES 6

BEEF WITH TOMATO & PEPPER IN BLACK BEAN SAUCE

Black beans are a specialty of Cantonese cooking
and give a pungent, salty taste to stir-fried dishes.

2 tbsps salted black beans
2 tbsps water
2 large tomatoes
4 tbsps dark soy sauce
1 tbsp cornstarch
1 tbsp dry sherry
1 tsp sugar
1lb rump steak, cut into thin strips
4 tbsps oil
1 small green pepper, seeded and cored
¾ cup beef stock
Pinch pepper

1. Core tomatoes and cut them into 16 wedges. Crush the black beans, add the water and set aside.

2. Combine soy sauce, cornstarch, sherry, sugar and meat in a bowl and set aside.

3. Cut pepper into ½ inch diagonal pieces. Heat the wok and add the oil. When hot, stir-fry the green pepper pieces for about 1 minute and remove.

4. Add the meat and the soy sauce mixture to the wok and stir-fry for about 2 minutes. Add the soaked black beans and the stock. Bring to the boil and allow to thicken slightly. Return the peppers to the wok and add the tomatoes and pepper. Heat through for 1 minute and serve immediately.

Step 1 Remove cores from the tomatoes with a sharp knife. Cut into even-sized wedges.

Step 4 Add the beef mixture to the hot wok and stir-fry until liquid ingredients glaze the meat.

Cook's Notes

 Time
Preparation takes about 25 minutes, cooking takes about 5 minutes.

 Serving Ideas
Serve with plain boiled rice.

 Watchpoint
Do not add the tomatoes too early or stir the mixture too vigorously once they are added or they will fall apart easily.

 Variation
Substitute pea pods for the green peppers in the recipe. Mushrooms may also be added and cooked with the peppers or pea pods.

SERVES 2-3

BEEF WITH BROCCOLI

The traditional Chinese method of cutting meat
for stir-frying used in this recipe ensures that
the meat will be tender and will cook quickly.

1lb rump steak, partially frozen
4 tbsps dark soy sauce
1 tbsp cornstarch
1 tbsp dry sherry
1 tsp sugar
8oz fresh broccoli
6 tbsps oil
1 inch piece ginger, peeled and shredded
Salt and pepper

1. Trim any fat from the meat and cut into very thin strips across the grain. Strips should be about 3 inches long.

2. Combine the meat with the soy sauce, cornstarch, sherry and sugar. Stir well and leave long enough for the meat to completely defrost.

3. Trim the flowerets from the stalks of the broccoli and cut them into even-sized pieces. Peel the stalks of the broccoli and cut into thin, diagonal slices.

4. Slice the ginger into shreds. Heat a wok and add 2 tbsps of the oil to it. Add the broccoli and sprinkle with salt. Stir-fry, turning constantly, until the broccoli is dark green. Do not cook for longer than 2 minutes. Remove from the wok and set aside.

5. Place the remaining oil in the wok and add the ginger and beef. Stir-fry, turning constantly, for about 2 minutes. Return the broccoli to the pan and mix well. Heat through for 30 seconds and serve immediately.

Step 1 Use partially frozen meat and slice it thinly across the grain.

Step 3 Cut the broccoli stalks in thin diagonal slices.

Step 4 To shred ginger quickly, cut into thin slices, stack up the slices and cut into thin strips.

Cook's Notes

 Time
Preparation takes about 25 minutes and cooking takes about 4 minutes.

 Preparation
Using meat that is partially frozen makes it easier to get very thin slices.

 Cook's Tip
If more sauce is desired, double the quantities of soy sauce, cornstarch, dry sherry and sugar.

SERVES 2-4

SWEET & SOUR PORK

This really needs no introduction because of its popularity. The dish originated in Canton, but is reproduced in most of the world's Chinese restaurants.

1 cup all-purpose flour
4 tbsps cornstarch
1½ tsps baking powder
Pinch salt
1 tbsp oil
Water
8oz pork tenderloin, cut into ½ inch cubes

Sweet and Sour Sauce

2 tbsps cornstarch
½ cup light brown sugar
Pinch salt
½ cup cider vinegar or rice vinegar
1 clove garlic, crushed
1 tsp fresh ginger, grated
6 tbsps tomato ketchup
6 tbsps reserved pineapple juice

1 onion, sliced
1 green pepper, seeded, cored and sliced
1 small can pineapple chunks, juice reserved
Oil for frying

1. To prepare the batter, sift the flour, cornstarch, baking powder and salt into a bowl. Make a well in the center and add the oil and enough water to make a thick, smooth batter. Using a wooden spoon, stir the ingredients in the well, gradually incorporating flour from the outside, and beat until smooth.

2. Heat enough oil in a wok to deep-fry the pork. Dip the pork cubes one at a time into the batter and drop into the hot oil. Fry 4-5 pieces of pork at a time and remove them with a draining spoon to paper towels. Continue until all the pork is fried.

3. Pour off most of the oil from the wok and add the sliced onion, pepper and pineapple. Cook over high heat for 1-2 minutes. Remove and set aside.

4. Mix all the sauce ingredients together and pour into the wok. Bring slowly to the boil, stirring continuously until thickened. Allow to simmer for about 1-2 minutes or until completely clear.

5. Add the vegetables, pineapple and pork cubes to the sauce and stir to coat completely. Reheat for 1-2 minutes and serve immediately.

Step 2 Dip the pork cubes into the batter and then drop into the hot oil. Chopsticks are ideal to use for this.

Step 3 Place the onion half flat on a chopping board and use a large, sharp knife to cut across to thick or thin slices as desired. Separate these into individual strips.

Cook's Notes

Time
Preparation takes about 15 minutes, cooking takes about 15 minutes.

Variation
Use beef or chicken instead of the pork. Uncooked, peeled shrimp may be used as can whitefish, cut into 1 inch pieces.

Cook's Tip
If pork is prepared ahead of time, this will have to be refried before serving to crisp up.

SERVES 4

CHICKEN LIVERS WITH CHINESE CABBAGE & ALMONDS

Chicken livers need quick cooking, so they are
a perfect choice for the Chinese stir-frying method.

8oz chicken livers
3 tbsps oil
½ cup split blanched almonds
1 clove garlic, peeled
2oz pea pods
8-10 Chinese cabbage leaves
2 tsps cornstarch mixed with 1 tbsp cold water
2 tbsps soy sauce
½ cup chicken stock

Step 2 Cook the almonds slowly in the oil to brown evenly, stirring often.

Step 1 Cut off any yellowish or greenish portions from the livers and divide them into even-sized pieces.

Step 3 Quickly stir-fry the livers until lightly browned on the outside. May be served slightly pink in the middle.

1. Pick over the chicken livers and remove any discolored areas or bits of fat. Cut the chicken livers into even-sized pieces.
2. Heat a wok and pour in the oil. When the oil is hot, turn the heat down and add the almonds. Cook, stirring continuously, over gentle heat until the almonds are a nice golden brown. Remove and drain on paper towels.
3. Add the garlic, cook for 1-2 minutes to flavor the oil and remove. Add the chicken livers and cook for about 2-3 minutes, stirring frequently. Remove the chicken livers and set them aside. Add the pea pods to the wok and stir-fry for 1 minute. Shred the Chinese cabbage leaves finely, add to the wok and cook for 1 minute. Remove the vegetables and set them aside.

4. Mix together the cornstarch and water with the soy sauce and stock. Pour into the wok and bring to the boil. Cook until thickened and clear. Return all the other ingredients to the sauce and reheat for 30 seconds. Serve immediately.

Cook's Notes

Time
Preparation takes about 25 minutes, cooking takes about 4-5 minutes.

Preparation
Remove any discolored portions from the livers as these can cause a bitter taste. Livers may be served slightly pink in the middle.

Serving Ideas
Serve with plain or fried rice. Chinese noodles also make a good accompaniment.

SERVES 4

CHICKEN WITH WALNUTS & CELERY

Oyster sauce lends a subtle, slightly
salty taste to this Cantonese dish.

8oz boned chicken, cut into 1 inch pieces
2 tsps soy sauce
2 tsps brandy
1 tsp cornstarch
Salt and pepper
2 tbsps oil
1 clove garlic
1 cup walnut halves
3 sticks celery, cut in diagonal slices
½ cup water or chicken stock
2 tsps oyster sauce

Step 3 Add the walnuts to the wok and cook until they are crisp.

Step 3 Cook the chicken until done but not brown.

Step 4 Use a large, sharp knife to cut the celery on the diagonal into thin slices.

1. Combine the chicken with the soy sauce, brandy, cornstarch, salt and pepper.

2. Heat a wok and add the oil and garlic. Cook for about 1 minute to flavor the oil.

3. Remove the garlic and add the chicken in two batches.

Stir-fry quickly without allowing the chicken to brown. Remove the chicken and add the walnuts to the wok. Cook for about 2 minutes until the walnuts are slightly brown and crisp.

4. Slice the celery, add to the wok and cook for about 1 minute. Add the oyster sauce and water and bring to the boil. When boiling, return the chicken to the pan and stir to coat all the ingredients well. Serve immediately.

Cook's Notes

Time
Preparation takes about 20 minutes, cooking takes about 8 minutes.

Watchpoint
Nuts can burn very easily. Stir them constantly for even browning.

Variation
Almonds or cashew nuts may be used instead of the walnuts. If the cashew nuts are already toasted, add them along with the celery.

Serving Ideas
Serve with boiled or fried rice.

Buying Guide
Oyster sauce, made from oysters and soy sauce, is available from Chinese supermarkets.

SERVES 6

CHICKEN WITH CLOUD EARS

Cloud ears is the delightful name
for an edible tree fungus which is
mushroom-like in taste and texture

12 cloud ears, wood ears or other dried Chinese
   mushrooms, soaked in boiling water for 5 minutes
1lb chicken breasts, boned and thinly sliced
1 egg white
2 tsps cornstarch
2 tsps white wine
2 tsps sesame oil
1 inch piece fresh ginger, left whole
1 clove garlic
1 cup oil
1 cup chicken stock
1 tbsp cornstarch
3 tbsps light soy sauce
Pinch salt and pepper

1. Soak the mushrooms until they soften and swell. Remove all the skin and bone from the chicken and cut it into thin slices. Mix the chicken with the egg white, cornstarch, wine and sesame oil.

2. Heat the wok for a few minutes and pour in the oil. Add the whole piece of ginger and whole garlic clove to the oil and cook for about 1 minute. Take them out and reduce the heat.

3. Add about a quarter of the chicken at a time and stir-fry for about 1 minute. Remove and continue cooking until all the chicken is fried. Remove all but about 2 tbsps of the oil from the wok.

4. Drain the mushrooms and squeeze them to extract all the liquid. If using mushrooms with stems, remove the stems before slicing thinly. Cut cloud ears or wood ears into smaller pieces. Add to the wok and cook for about 1 minute. Add the stock and allow it to come almost to the boil. Mix together the cornstarch and soy sauce and add a spoonful of the hot stock. Add the mixture to the wok, stirring constantly, and bring to the boil. Allow to boil 1-2 minutes or until thickened. The sauce will clear when the cornstarch has cooked sufficiently.

5. Return the chicken to the wok and add salt and pepper. Stir thoroughly for about 1 minute and serve immediately.

Step 1 Soak the cloud ears or mushrooms in boiling water for five minutes, they will swell in size.

Step 3 Stir-fry the chicken in small batches, placing in the oil with chopsticks.

Cook's Notes

Time
Preparation takes about 25 minutes, cooking takes about 5 minutes.

Preparation
If desired, the chicken may be cut into 1 inch cubes. If slicing, cut across the grain as this helps the chicken to cook more evenly.

Variation
Flat, cup or button mushrooms may be used instead of the dried mushrooms. Eliminate the soaking and slice them thickly. Cook as for the dried variety. 2 tsps bottled oyster sauce may be added with the stock.

Buying Guide
Cloud ears or wood ears are a type of edible Chinese tree fungus. They are both available from Chinese supermarkets and some delicatessens. Chinese mushrooms are more readily available. Both keep a long time in their dried state. Chinese ingredients are becoming more readily available. Check supermarket shelves for bottled sauces like Oyster Sauce.

SERVES 4

Spun Fruits

Often called toffee fruits, this sweet
consists of fruit fried in batter and
coated with a thin, crisp caramel glaze.

Batter

1 cup all-purpose flour, sifted
Pinch salt
1 egg
½ cup water and milk mixed half and half
Oil for deep frying

Caramel Syrup

1 cup sugar
3 tbsps water
1 tbsp oil
1 large apple, peeled, cored and cut into 2 inch chunks
1 banana, peeled and cut into 1 inch pieces
Ice water

1. To prepare the batter, combine all the ingredients, except the oil for deep frying, in a liquidizer or food processor and process to blend. Pour into a bowl and dip in the prepared fruit.

2. In a heavy-based saucepan, combine the sugar with the water and oil and cook over very low heat until the sugar dissolves. Bring to the boil and allow to cook rapidly until a pale caramel color.

3. While the sugar is dissolving, heat the oil in a wok and fry the batter-dipped fruit, a few pieces at a time.

4. While the fruit is still hot and crisp, use chopsticks or a pair of tongs to dip the fruit into the hot caramel syrup. Stir each piece around to coat evenly.

5. Dip immediately into ice water to harden the syrup and place each piece on a greased dish. Continue cooking all the fruit in the same way.

6. Once the caramel has hardened and the fruit has cooled, transfer to a clean serving plate.

Step 2 Cook the syrup until the sugar dissolves and is a pale golden brown.

Step 4 Using tongs or chopsticks, immediately dip the fried fruit into the hot syrup, swirling to coat evenly.

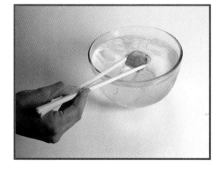

Step 5 Dip the caramel coated fruit into ice water to harden. Place on a greased dish to cool.

Cook's Notes

Time
Preparation takes about 25 minutes, cooking takes from 10-15 minutes.

Variation
Lychees may be used either fresh or canned. Organization is very important for the success of this dish. Have the batter ready, syrup prepared, fruit sliced and ice water on hand before beginning.

Watchpoint
Watch the syrup carefully and do not allow it to become too brown. This will give a bitter taste to the dish.

MAKES 30 COOKIES

ALMOND COOKIES

In China these are often eaten as a
between-meal snack. In Western style cuisine, they
make a good accompaniment to fruit or sorbet.

1 stick butter or margarine
4 tbsps granulated sugar
2 tbsps light brown sugar
1 egg, beaten
Almond extract
1 cup all-purpose flour
1 tsp baking powder
Pinch salt
¼ cup ground almonds, blanched or unblanched
2 tbsps water
30 whole blanched almonds

Step 2 Add egg and flavoring and beat until smooth.

Step 3 Shape into small balls with floured hands on a floured surface. Place well apart on baking sheets.

Step 1 Cream the butter and sugars until light and fluffy.

1. Cream the butter or margarine together with the two sugars until light and fluffy.

2. Divide the beaten egg in half and add half to the sugar mixture with a few drops of the almond extract and beat until smooth. Reserve the remaining egg for later use. Sift the flour, baking powder and salt into the egg mixture and add the ground almonds. Stir well by hand.

3. Shape the mixture into small balls and place well apart on a lightly greased baking sheet. Flatten slightly and press an almond on to the top of each one.

4. Mix the reserved egg with the water and brush each cookie before baking.

5. Place in a preheated 350°F oven and bake for 12-15 minutes. Cookies will be a pale golden color when done.

Cook's Notes

 Time
Preparation takes about 10 minutes. If the dough becomes too soft, refrigerate for 10 minutes before shaping. Cooking takes about 12-15 minutes per batch.

 Cook's Tip
Roll the mixture on a floured surface with floured hands to prevent sticking.

 Watchpoint
Do not over beat once the almonds are added. They will begin to oil and the mixture will become too soft and sticky to shape.

 Serving Ideas
Serve with fruit, ice cream or sorbet. Do not reserve just for Chinese meals.

 Freezing
Cookies may be frozen baked or unbaked. Defrost uncooked dough completely at room temperature before baking. Baked cookies may be re-crisped by heating in the oven for about 2 minutes and then allowed to cool before serving.

SERVES 6

Sweet Bean Wontons

Wonton snacks, either sweet or savory, are another popular tea house treat. Made from prepared wonton wrappers and ready-made bean paste, these couldn't be more simple.

15 wonton wrappers
8oz sweet red bean paste
1 tbsp cornstarch
4 tbsps cold water
Oil for deep frying
Honey

1. Take a wonton wrapper in the palm of your hand and place a little of the red bean paste slightly above the center.

2. Mix together the cornstarch and water and moisten the edge around the filling.

3. Fold over, slightly off center.

4. Pull the sides together, using the cornstarch and water paste to stick the two together.

5. Turn inside out by gently pushing the filled center.

6. Heat enough oil in a wok for deep-fat frying and when hot, put in 4 of the filled wontons at a time. Cook until crisp and golden and remove to paper towels to drain. Repeat with the remaining filled wontons. Serve drizzled with honey.

Step 4 Bring the two sides together and stick with cornstarch and water paste.

Step 5 Push the filled portion gently through the middle to turn inside out.

Cook's Notes

Variation
Add a small amount of grated ginger to the red bean paste for a slight change in flavor. Wontons may also be sprinkled with sugar instead of honey.

Buying Guide
Wontons, wonton wrappers and red bean paste are available in Chinese supermarkets.

SERVES 6-8

ALMOND FLOAT WITH FRUIT

Sweet dishes are not often served in the course
of a Chinese meal. Banquets are the exception, and
this elegant fruit salad is certainly special enough.

1 envelope unflavored gelatine
6 tbsps cold water
⅓ cup sugar
1 cup milk
1 tsp almond extract
Few drops red or yellow food coloring (optional)

Almond Sugar Syrup

⅓ cup sugar
2 cups water
½ tsp almond extract

Fresh fruit such as kiwi, mango, pineapple, bananas,
    lychees, oranges or satsumas, peaches, berries,
    cherries, grapes or starfruit
Fresh mint for garnish

1. Allow the gelatine to soften in the cold water for about 10 minutes or until spongy. Put in a large mixing bowl.

2. Bring ⅓ cup water to the boil and stir in the sugar. Pour into the gelatine and water mixture and stir until gelatine and sugar dissolves.

3. Add milk, flavoring and food coloring if using. Mix well and pour into an 8 inch square pan. Chill in the refrigerator until set.

4. Mix the sugar and water for the syrup together in a heavy-based pan. Cook over gentle heat until the sugar dissolves. Bring to the boil and allow to boil for about 2 minutes, or until the syrup thickens slightly. Add the almond extract and allow to cool at room temperature. Chill in the refrigerator until ready to use.

5. Prepare the fruit and place in attractive serving dish. Pour over the chilled syrup and mix well.

6. Cut the set almond float into 1 inch diamond shapes or cubes. Use a spatula to remove them from the pan and stir them gently into the fruit mixture. Decorate with sprigs of fresh mint to serve.

Step 2 Add boiling water and sugar, and stir until the mixture is clear and not grainy.

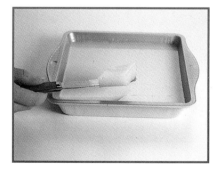

Step 6 Cut the set almond float mixture into cubes and remove from the pan with a palette knife.

Cook's Notes

Time
Preparation takes about 25 minutes. The almond float will need about 2 hours to set.

Preparation
To prepare kiwi fruit, peel with a swivel vegetable peeler and cut into thin rounds. To prepare lychees, peel off the rough outer skin. Cut around the stone or leave it in. To prepare mangoes, peel and cut into thin slices around the large stone. To prepare starfruit, wash and cut crosswise into thin slices. The shape of the slices will resemble a star.

Buying Guide
Use whatever fruits are in season at the moment, or use good quality canned fruit. Exotic fruits are available in most large supermarkets and some greengrocers. Allow about 2lbs of fruit for 6-8 people.

INDEX

ACKNOWLEDGMENT
The publishers wish to thank the following suppliers
for their kind assistance:
Corning Ltd for providing Pyrex and other cookware.
Habasco International Ltd for the loan of basketware.
Stent (Pottery) Ltd for the loan of glazed pottery oven-
to-table ware.

Compiled by Judith Ferguson
Photographed by Peter Barry
Designed by Philip Clucas and Sara Cooper
Recipes Prepared for Photography by
Jacqueline Bellefontaine